First World War
and Army of Occupation
War Diary
France, Belgium and Germany

46 DIVISION
Divisional Troops
Royal Army Medical Corps
Divisional Field Ambulance Workshop Unit
16 February 1915 - 31 January 1916

WO95/2681/2

The Naval & Military Press Ltd
www.nmarchive.com
Published in association with The National Archives

Published by

The Naval & Military Press Ltd

Unit 10 Ridgewood Industrial Park,

Uckfield, East Sussex,

TN22 5QE England

Tel: +44 (0) 1825 749494

www.naval-military-press.com

www.nmarchive.com

This diary has been reprinted in facsimile from the original. Any imperfections are inevitably reproduced and the quality may fall short of modern type and cartographic standards.

© **Crown Copyright**
Images reproduced by permission of The National Archives, London, England, 2015.

Contents

Document type	Place/Title	Date From	Date To
Heading	46th Division Medical Nth Mid'd Fd Amb. W' Shop Unit Feb 1915-Apr 1916.		
Heading	BEF 46 Division 46 Ambulance Workshop 1915 Nov-1916 Apr.		
War Diary	Bavinchove.	01/03/1915	06/03/1915
War Diary	Grove Park.	16/02/1915	20/02/1915
War Diary	Bulford.	21/02/1915	22/02/1915
War Diary	Avonmouth	23/02/1915	25/02/1915
War Diary	Bailleul.	12/03/1915	12/03/1915
War Diary	Sailly	13/03/1915	15/03/1915
War Diary	Gaestre.	16/03/1915	21/03/1915
War Diary	Bavinchove.	07/03/1915	08/03/1915
War Diary	Praddles.	09/03/1915	10/03/1915
War Diary	Sailly.	11/03/1915	11/03/1915
War Diary	Bailleul	12/03/1915	12/03/1915
War Diary	Southampton	25/02/1915	26/02/1915
War Diary	Havre	26/02/1915	26/02/1915
War Diary	Rouen.	27/02/1915	28/02/1915
War Diary	Gosnay.	21/11/1915	25/11/1915
War Diary	Locon.	26/11/1915	26/11/1915
War Diary	Sheet No. 19 Poperinghe.	28/08/1915	31/08/1915
War Diary	Sheet No.18. Poperinghe.	16/08/1915	27/08/1915
War Diary	Gosnay	05/11/1915	20/11/1915
War Diary	Doullens.	01/03/1916	05/03/1916
War Diary	Le Cauroy.	06/03/1916	10/03/1916
War Diary	Camblain L'Abbe	11/03/1916	11/03/1916
War Diary	St. Vennant.	10/12/1915	15/12/1915
War Diary	Marseilles.	21/01/1916	26/01/1916
War Diary	on Rail.	27/01/1916	28/01/1916
War Diary	Pont Remy.	29/01/1916	30/01/1916
War Diary	St. Vennant.	16/12/1915	19/12/1915
War Diary	Thiennes	20/12/1915	22/12/1915
War Diary	Mingoval.	12/03/1916	21/03/1916
War Diary	St. Vennant.	10/12/1915	15/12/1915
War Diary	L.12.a.N.W. Sheet 27. 1:/40,000.	26/07/1915	31/07/1915
War Diary	St Vennant.	08/12/1915	09/12/1915
War Diary	La Haie Farm.	15/02/1916	20/02/1916
War Diary	Bernaville.	21/02/1916	26/02/1916
War Diary	Locon.	01/12/1915	06/12/1915
War Diary	St. Vennant.	07/12/1915	07/12/1915
War Diary	Ailly-Haut-Clocher.	08/02/1916	11/02/1916
War Diary	La Haie Farm.	12/02/1916	14/02/1916
War Diary	Sheet No. 12. St. Jans Cappel.	16/06/1915	25/06/1915
War Diary	St. Jans Cappel.	26/06/1915	28/06/1915
War Diary	Sheet No. 14. St. Jans Cappel.	01/07/1915	07/07/1915
War Diary	Sheet 27.L.23.b. N.E.1/40,000.	07/07/1915	12/07/1915
War Diary	St. Vennant.	08/12/1915	09/12/1915
War Diary	Le Harvre.	01/01/1916	06/01/1916
War Diary	On Rail.	07/01/1916	08/01/1916
War Diary	Marseilles.	09/01/1916	09/01/1916

War Diary	St. Vennant	16/12/1915	19/12/1915
War Diary	Thiennes	20/12/1915	22/12/1915
War Diary	Marseilles	10/01/1916	20/01/1916
War Diary	Mingoval.	22/03/1916	31/03/1916
War Diary	Gosnay	05/11/1915	20/11/1915
War Diary	Sheet 27.1/40000 L. 29. ab.	01/09/1915	14/09/1915
War Diary	St. Jans. Capelle.	16/04/1915	30/04/1915
War Diary	Sheet No. 17. Poperinghe.	01/08/1915	15/08/1915
War Diary	Caestre.	22/03/1915	31/03/1915
War Diary	Ailly-Le-Haut Clocher.	01/02/1916	07/02/1916
War Diary	Le Harvre.	01/01/1916	06/01/1916
War Diary	On Rail.	07/01/1916	08/01/1916
War Diary	Marseilles	09/01/1916	09/01/1916
War Diary	Bernaville	27/02/1916	29/02/1916
War Diary	St. Jans Cappel.	29/06/1915	30/06/1915
War Diary	Doullens.	01/03/1916	05/03/1916
War Diary	Le Cauroy.	06/03/1916	10/03/1916
War Diary	Camblain L'Abbe.	11/03/1916	11/03/1916
War Diary	Locon.	27/11/1915	30/11/1915
War Diary	Ailly-Le Haut-Clocher.	01/02/1916	07/02/1916
War Diary	La Haie Farm.	15/02/1916	20/02/1916
War Diary	Bernaville.	21/02/1916	26/02/1916
War Diary	Ailly-Le-Haut-Clocher.	08/02/1916	11/02/1916
War Diary	La Haie Farm.	12/02/1916	14/02/1916
War Diary	Bernaville	27/02/1916	29/02/1916
War Diary	Sheet 27 1/40000 L. 29. ab.	15/09/1915	30/09/1915
War Diary	Caestre.	01/04/1915	09/04/1915
War Diary	St Jans. Capelle.	09/04/1915	15/04/1915
War Diary	Thiennes	23/12/1915	23/12/1915
War Diary	Abbeville.	24/12/1915	24/12/1915
War Diary	Neuchatel	25/12/1915	25/12/1915
War Diary	Le Harvre.	26/12/1915	31/12/1915
War Diary	Locon.	01/12/1915	06/12/1915
War Diary	St. Vennant.	07/12/1915	07/12/1915
War Diary	Mingoval	12/03/1916	21/03/1916
War Diary	St. Jans. Cappel.	16/05/1916	31/05/1916
War Diary	Mingoval.	22/03/1916	31/03/1916
War Diary	Marseilles.	21/01/1916	26/01/1916
War Diary	On Rail.	27/01/1916	28/01/1916
War Diary	Pont Remy.	29/01/1916	30/01/1916
War Diary	Sheet 27 L.23.B.NE. 1/40,000.	13/07/1915	26/07/1915
War Diary	Marseilles.	10/01/1916	20/01/1916
War Diary	Gosnay.	21/11/1915	25/11/1915
War Diary	Locon.	26/11/1915	26/11/1915
War Diary	St. Jans Cappel.	01/06/1915	15/06/1915
War Diary	Locon.	27/11/1915	30/11/1915
War Diary	Ailly-Le-Haut Clocher.	31/01/1916	31/01/1916
War Diary	Mingoval	01/04/1916	06/04/1916
War Diary	Thiennes	23/12/1915	23/12/1915
War Diary	Abbeville.	24/12/1915	24/12/1915
War Diary	Neuchatel.	25/12/1915	25/12/1915
War Diary	Le Harvre.	26/12/1915	31/12/1915
War Diary	St. Jans Cappel.	01/05/1915	15/05/1915
War Diary	Mingoval	01/04/1916	06/04/1916
War Diary	Ailly-Le-Haut-Clocher.	31/01/1916	31/01/1916
Heading	46 Div Fa Lieut Workshop Jan Vol XI Jan 1916.		

Heading	46th Division 46 F.A.W.U. Vol IX 121/7694 Nov 15.
Heading	46th Div F.A.W.U. Dec Vol XI 121/7929 Dec 1915.
Heading	121/4538 Feb 16th 1915 N.M. Field Ambulance Workshop Unit Vol II Feb 1915.
Heading	46th Division 46th Div F.A. Workshop Unit Vol VII August 15.
Heading	War Diary Of 46th Divisional Field Ambulance Workshop Unit. A.S.C. March For April 1916.
Heading	WO/2681/2.
Heading	46th Division 46th Field Amb Workshop Unit Vol VI July 1915.
Heading	46th Division 46th M Amb Workshop Unit Vol VIII Sept 15.
Heading	46th (N.lb) F.A.W.U. Feb 1916.
Heading	121/5195 April 1915 Mortar Midland Fl Amb Workshop Vol III 121/5195.
Heading	46th Divl Field Ambulance Workshop Unit Vol IV May 1915.
Heading	N.M. Division 46th North Midland Fld Ambulance Workshop Vol II 1-31.3.15.
Heading	46th Division 46th Divl F.A. Workshop Vol V June 1915.
Heading	Fd Amb Work Unit Vol XIV.
Heading	46th Fd Amb Work Unit Vol I.

46TH DIVISION
MEDICAL

NTH MID'D FD AMB. W'SHOP UNIT

FEB 1915-APR 1916

46TH DIVISION
MEDICAL

BEF

46 DIVISION

46 ~~FIELD~~ AMBULANCE WORKSHOP

1915 NOV — 1916 APL

O/C. North Midland
Field Ambulance &
Workshop Unit.

WAR DIARY

INTELLIGENCE SUMMARY

(Erase heading not required.)

Army Form C. 2118.

Place	Date	Hour	Summary of Events and Information	Remarks and references to Appendices
Page No 1.				
Bavinchove	1/3/15	8.30 p.m.	Myself and Unit left Abbeville according to Orders received from D.A.Q.M.G. 46th Batt. Abbeville, at 8.30 and proceeded to Bavinchove. We arrived at BAVINCHOVE at 6.30 p.m. Reported myself to H.Q N. Mid. Division.	
BAVINCHOVE	2/3/15	7.30 P.M.	According to Orders received from Cpt. Darcy, I sent 2 Ambulances to the Notts & Derby Brigade, for General duty.	
"	3/3/15	8 P.M.	I reported myself to Col. Benoit, A.D.M.S. North. Mid. Div. 3 of my Men reported sick and were sent to Hospital at St. Omer in accordance with instructions received from Col. Benoit.	
"	4/3/15	8.30 P.M.	I proceeded to Dieppe with Col. Benoit, the Unit remaining at Bavinchove.	
"	5/3/15	7.30 P.M.	One Ambulance W.O. No. returned from Notts & Derby Brig. with rear Drum broken. Such repairs as were possible were done & another Ambulance sent in place of No.	
"	6/3/15	7.30 P.M.	I remained at BAVINCHOVE waiting for orders	

Army Form C. 2118.

Sheet 1

Instructions regarding War Diaries and Intelligence Summaries are contained in F.S. Regs., Part II. and the Staff Manual respectively. Title pages will be prepared in manuscript.

WAR DIARY
or
INTELLIGENCE SUMMARY.

(Erase heading not required.)

Summary of Events and Information

Place	Date	Hour	Summary of Events and Information	Remarks and references to Appendices
Grove Park	16/2/15		I received Orders from Major Pennington, A.S.C. to Mobilise the North Midland Field Ambulance & Workshops Unit.	
"	17/2/15		I proceeded to Woolwich & drew Ordnance Stores.	
"	18/2/15		I proceeded to Aldershot & drew M.T.V. Stores.	
"	19/2/15		I got my Unit together generally today.	
"	20/2/15		I received Orders at 2.30 p.m. Proceed to Bulford.	
Bulford	21/2/15		I arrived Bulford at 5.30 p.m.	
"	22/2/15		I left Bulford at 12. noon for Avonmouth.	
Avonmouth	23/2/15	At 11.30 p.m.	I started having my Vehicles placed on Board the "S.S. Balmoral" This was finished at 4.30. Arrived here at 10.30 p.m.	
"	24/2/15		Remained with my Men on board until 9.45 p.m when I received Orders to leave 4 men & 1. N.C.O on Board & the rest were to be taken to Station at Avonmouth.	
"	25/2/15		Train left for Southampton at 1.30 A.M. & arr. Southampton at 4.30 A.M. On Arr. Pte. G.W. Grayne reported sick & was taken to Hospital at Southampton. (N° 04 8079)	

Army Form C. 2118.

WAR DIARY
or
INTELLIGENCE SUMMARY.
(Erase heading not required.)

Instructions regarding War Diaries and Intelligence Summaries are contained in F. S. Regs., Part II and the Staff Manual respectively. Title pages will be prepared in manuscript.

Sheet N° 6.

Place	Date	Hour	Summary of Events and Information	Remarks and references to Appendices
BAILLEUL	12/3/15	7.30.	Drew and packed in the square	
SAILLY.	13/3/15.		Received orders by Telegram at 8.p.m. Last night to proceed at once to Sailly with Convoy. Left at 8.10.p.m. and arrived at SAILLY at 10.30 p.m. Remained all day at SAILLY awaiting orders	
"	14/3/15.	8.p.m.	Stayed all day at SAILLY. The Ambulances carried a few sick to Hospital.	
"	15/3/15.		Awaited Orders all day to move.	
CAESTRE	16/3/15.		Received orders this morning from the A.D.M.S. to proceed to CAESTRE about 1.30.p.m. This I did and arrived here at 3.45. p.m. I Parked in a square & remained for the night. Remained at CAESTRE waiting for orders.	
"	17/3/15		ditto	
"	18/3/15		ditto — and carried out necessary repairs to Ambulances	
"	19/3/15		ditto —	
"	20/3/15		ditto —	
"	21/3/15		ditto —. A German Aeroplane dropped a bomb not far from us my party.	

Army Form C. 2118.

WAR DIARY
or
INTELLIGENCE SUMMARY.
(Erase heading not required.)

Instructions regarding War Diaries and Intelligence Summaries are contained in F. S. Regs., Part II. and the Staff Manual respectively. Title pages will be prepared in manuscript.

Place	Date	Hour	Summary of Events and Information	Remarks and references to Appendices
Sheet	No 4.			
BAVINCHOVE	7/3/15	4.15 P.M.	I drove Col. Beevor to HAZEBROUCK and returned to BAVINCHOVE.	
"	8/3/15	7. P.M.	S.ted by awaiting orders. Received orders from Col. Beevor A.D.M.S to send 2 (two) Ambulances to 2nd North Mid. Field Ambulance Section at ZUYTPEENE for general duty. This order was carried out. Received orders to hand over Rifles of Ambulance trains to Major Kelly. (D.D.O.S. North Mid. Div). This was done and a receipt got for same received.	
PRADELLES	9/3/15	7.30 p/m.	Received Orders this morning to proceed with Convoy to PRADELLES. I arrived there at 4.30. The Ambulances were distributed to their different Field Ambulance Units. Remained at PRADELLES today.	
"	10/3/15			
SAILLY	11/3/15		Received orders to proceed with Ambulances on the road to Sailly. I went there personally and the Unit remained about 3 miles outside all night.	
BAILLEUL	12/3/15		Received orders to take Convoy to BAILLEUL. I proceeded	

Army Form C. 2118.

WAR DIARY
or
INTELLIGENCE SUMMARY.
(Erase heading not required.)

Instructions regarding War Diaries and Intelligence Summaries are contained in F. S. Regs., Part II. and the Staff Manual respectively. Title pages will be prepared in manuscript.

Place	Date	Hour	Summary of Events and Information	Remarks and references to Appendices
Southampton	25/2/15		We went on Board the S.S. Empress Queen about 5 o'clock p.m.	
	26/2/15		We arrived at Havre at early in the morning & disembarked at 9 A.M. We went on board the "S/S King Edward" at 2.p.m. & left for Rouen at 4.15, arriving there 10.30. We slept the night on the boat.	
Rouen	27/2/15		We disembarked at 8.30 & waited the arrival of the "S.S. Palacrat." This boat arrived about 4.p.m. Unloading vehicles & was at once started & was finished about 11.30 p.m.	
Rouen	28/2/15		I received orders to proceed to Abbeville at 12. noon. & arrived at Abbeville at 10.30. I reported to the Commandant & to the D.D.T. Abbeville with my unit. I started	

G.G. Burwash
Lieut. A.S.C. M.T.
O.C. North Midland Field Ambulance & Workshops Unit.

28/2/15

WAR DIARY
or
INTELLIGENCE SUMMARY

Army Form C. 2118

Place	Date	Hour	Summary of Events and Information	Remarks and references to Appendices
GOSNAY	21.11.15		Routine work. Dainton car which was overhauled while I was on leave was found to have a broken differential casing. Car consequently out of action waiting for new part.	
"	22.11.15		Visited No 1 & 3 Field Ambulances & instructed the sergeants as to making returns of the doings of Ambulances. Went to see the ADMS at LESTREM but he was out. Saw E ISEBERG & obtained a piece of steel to make a back axle sleeve of one of the Sunbeam Ambulances, the car having been out of action for very many weeks waiting for a new part from the Base MT depot. Instructed the sergeant to have lighted lamps placed under the bonnets of the Ambulances to guard against frost.	
"	23.11.15		Routine work	
"	24.11.15		Routine work. Paid the Sunbeam Ambulance complete	
"	25.11.15		Received instructions at 11 o'clock to move the new S & the MERVILLE. Called on Major Preston at LESTREM who suggested my calling on Major Potter of the supply column with regard to finding a suitable situation. Called on Major Potter + searched all round MERVILLE but could find no suitable moveable place. Later the ADMS suggested a farm at LOCON which I found very suitable. BETHUNE confirmed mat. X7d7.7. Sunbeam Ambulance complete + on road.	
LOCON	26.11.15		Drew money from field cashier at MERVILLE. Paid 1 & a 3rd Field Ambulance. Fitted up the workshop to dig pit etc in the new place.	

WAR DIARY
INTELLIGENCE SUMMARY.
(Erase heading not required.)

Army Form C. 2118.

Place	Date	Hour	Summary of Events and Information	Remarks and references to Appendices
Sheet No. 19.				
POPERINGHE	28.8.15		Usual daily routine, weather fine & warm.	
	29.8.15		" " " " Weather wet and much colder.	
	30.8.15		" " " to 9a.m. asked by the Town Major to move out of this place as it was wanted for Hosps. 9 reported this to Headquarters & proceeded to find another suitable place in our area.	
	31.8.15		Usual Routine. One of my Ambulances was reported to me, that as touring being badly hit by Shrapnel on its way to Three Kings on the YPRES - LILLE ROAD. No damage was done to the Chassis, only the body work, badly torn. From the drivers report, I gathered that the Ambulance was deliberately shelled by the Germans, as it had to pace along a road partially in view of the Enemy lines. The driver were uninjured.	

G. G. Durward
G. G. Durward
2/L. A.S.C. O.C. 46 H. Div. F.A.W.U.

Army Form C. 2118

WAR DIARY
or
INTELLIGENCE SUMMARY.
(Erase heading not required.)

Instructions regarding War Diaries and Intelligence Summaries are contained in F. S. Regs., Part II. and the Staff Manual respectively. Title pages will be prepared in manuscript.

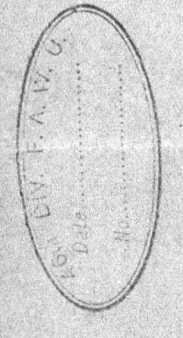

Place	Date	Hour	Summary of Events and Information	Remarks and references to Appendices
Sheet No. 18.				
POPERINGHE	16.8.15		Received carrying & necessary repairs out.	
"	17.8.15		Shelled today. Weather fine.	
"	18.8.15		Carried out usual daily routine.	
"	19.8.15		" " " " " " Weather still fine.	
"	20.8.15		" " " " " " " "	
"	21.8.15		" " " " " " " "	
"	22.8.15		" " " " " " Shells fell in POPERINGHE at different times nearly all day & several enemy aeroplanes passed over.	
"	23.8.15		Usual daily routine.	
"	24.8.15		" " "	
"	25.8.15		" " " Big shells again dropped just outside the town. Very little damage done.	
"	26.8.15		Usual daily routine. Weather fine & very warm	
"	27.8.15		" " " " " "	

1577 Wt. W10791/1773 500,000 1/15 D.D. & L. A.D.S.S./Forms/C. 2118.

WAR DIARY or INTELLIGENCE SUMMARY

Army Form C. 2118

Place	Date	Hour	Summary of Events and Information	Remarks and references to Appendices
GOSNAY	5.11.15		I left the 15th Divisional Supply Column which was parked at LILLERS & joined my new unit, the 40th Divisional Field Ambulance & Workshop Unit & reported to A.D.M.S. Col Beevor. The workshops are billeted in the school yard at GOSNAY. Called on Major Turner & inspected the ambulances of the 2nd Field Ambulance at VERQUIN	
"	6.11.15		Went with ADMS to Div H.Q. at LESTREM. Went on to ST. OMER & obtained a new radiator for his Daimler car	
"	7.11.15		Searched for a suitable billet for the workshops in the new Divisional area. Called at Div HQ & the ADMS & arranged to defer moving from the present position for the time being.	
"	8.11.15		Called upon ADMS at LESTREM & ascertained the position of the field Ambulances. Drew 6840 francs to pay from the field cashier at VAUDRICOURT. Paid the workshop men.	
"	9.11.15		Visited the 1st NM Field Ambulance at VIELLE CHAPPELLE, the 2nd do. at BUSNES & the 3rd do. at ZELOBES. Paid the men at all three places, inspected the ambulances & impressed upon the sergeants the necessity for great cleanliness. Called on the ADMS at LESTREM.	
"	10.11.15		Went to England on leave	
"	20.11.15		Returned from leave	

Army Form C. 2118.

WAR DIARY
or
INTELLIGENCE SUMMARY.
(Erase heading not required.)

Instructions regarding War Diaries and Intelligence Summaries are contained in F.S. Regs., Part II. and the Staff Manual respectively. Title pages will be prepared in manuscript.

Place	Date	Hour	Summary of Events and Information	Remarks and references to Appendices
DOULLENS	1.3.16		Left BERNAVILLE at 9 A.M. with lorries & Ambulances under repair & went to DOULLENS. Placed workshops in the MARCHE' AU BLÉ	
"	2.3.16		Ordinary routine	
"	3.3.16		" "	
"	4.3.16		" "	
"	5.3.16		Called on 1/1st & 1/2nd Field Ambulances at BEAUVAL. Received order from ADMS & went to LE CAUROY on the following day, leaving not later than 1.4.16.	
LE CAUROY	6.3.16		In the morning went to LE CAUROY & fixed position for the unit with the Camp Commandant. In the afternoon brought unit from DOULLENS to LE CAUROY	
"	7.3.16		Ordinary routine	
"	8.3.16		Sent to DOULLENS to see a broken down ambulance. Went again in the afternoon to obtain a new cylinder head for Sanitary lorry from Supply Column. Sunbeam Ambulance A15187 broke off drawbar	
"	9.3.16		Sent to Supply Column at AUBIGNY to find out what had become of tyres which had arrived by rail.	
"	10.3.16		Ordinary routine. Received orders to move to CAMBLAIN L'ABBE next day afters 12 midday. Sunbeam Ambulance A15327 broke its crown wheel.	
CAMBLAIN L'ABBE	11.3.16		Moved to CAMBLAIN L'ABBE & parked lorries & cars in the street. Sunbeam Ambulance A17707 broke its crown wheel. Sunbeam Ambulance 9564 had a bad skid damaging back axle, frame body etc	

Army Form C. 2118.

WAR DIARY
or
INTELLIGENCE SUMMARY.
(Erase heading not required.)

Instructions regarding War Diaries and Intelligence Summaries are contained in F.S. Regs., Part II. and the Staff Manual respectively. Title pages will be prepared in manuscript.

Place	Date	Hour	Summary of Events and Information	Remarks and references to Appendices
ST. VENANT	10.12.15		Exchanged R 3 Fd Ambce Star lorry for a Peerless star lorry in R square of MERVILLE. Exchanged R Scouts car for a sunken car from R John FA WH in R Sqre of LILLERS. Received orders from DDMS 1st Army RC 12 Refrs	
"	11.12.15		Ambulance was Re exchanged for a sunken from R 14th Divn Fd Ambu. Took Re exchanged lorries Ambulance R to Tobacco factory at LOCON & exchanged " for a sunken from R 19th Divn FA WH. This completed all R exchanges directed to be carried out. In every case the drivers were retained in their respective unit. Received a consignment of 9 drivers which Huggins arranged to be established.	
"	12.12.15		Inspected men (horses) of 2nd NM Field Ambulance & also workshop men who were not always the Dvnl though all R Methods - received very necessary attention	
"	13.12.15		Went to STEENBECQUE - stood spring test. Visited the 3rd NM Fd Ambulance	
"	14.12.15		Went to ISBERGUES & got Mr Q to be call for one of R Ford Ambulances they already & made the Journey R R. Turn taken in detaining officer from R here. Obtained money for field clothes of MERVILLE & paid the drivers of R 2nd & 3rd NM Field ambulances accordingly been	
"	15.12.15		Paid drivers of 1st NMFA. Went with R ADMS R road to return to home LESTREM DESGUETTE	

WAR DIARY
or
INTELLIGENCE SUMMARY.

Army Form C. 2118.

Place	Date	Hour	Summary of Events and Information	Remarks and references to Appendices
MARSEILLES	21.1.16		Sent 7 ambulances to take sitting cases & the dock & for embarkation	
"	22.1.16		Sent 5 ambulances to bring the sitting cases back again.	
"	23.1.16		Drew orders from Base Cashier & paid the men.	
"	24.1.16		Ordinary routine. Put Sergt H Davidson under arrest for drunkenness & insolence	
"	25.1.16		" took 7 ambulances to station in evening & entrain with 1st N.M. Field ambulance.	
"	26.1.16		Received orders during the afternoon for entrain for entrain on train leaving at 3.12 next morning. Arranged with DADRT & have trucks in readiness under electric crane for loading the lorries & the ambulances of 3rd N.M. Field ambulance going by same train. Left for ARENC station at 10.15.	
On Rail	27.1.16		Informed that crane was out of order. Two of the lorries having to be loaded with their bodies on a separate truck on account of too great height, the lorries had to be left behind, & having arranged this they were to come on next morning. Still loaded the ambulances. Train left 5.30 A.M.	
"	28.1.16		Journey continued	
PONT REMY	29.1.16		Arrived at PONT REMY at 5.30 A.M. Unloaded ambulances. Billeted the men. Handed over to Serjeant under arrest to K. A.P.M. Went with Col. Wark to the 3rd & 1st N.M. Field ambulance.	
"	30.1.16		Lorries arrived about 2 A.M. but there being no tackle for unloading them the trucks were sent on to ABBEVILLE with a fatigue party until 1 p.m. Went to SAILLY-LE-HAUT-CLOCHER & secured a place for the HS	

Army Form C. 2118.

WAR DIARY
or
INTELLIGENCE SUMMARY.
(Erase heading not required.)

Place	Date	Hour	Summary of Events and Information	Remarks and references to Appendices
ST. VENNANT	16/12/15		LILLERS in view of having entrainment at base stations. Went to LILLERS & found out what tables was available for lifting the bodies of workshop & store lorries on to railway trucks. Two M.T. drivers arrived from ROUEN.	
"	17/12/15		General routine work.	
"	18/12/15		Received information as to move on the following day. W/d C. THIENNES & noted the place. Sgt James arrived from G.H.Q. a base & 3rd N.M. field ambulance.	
"	19/12/15		Moved to THIENNES & fixed the workshops in the square. Unable to find a more suitable place which was not already taken.	
THIENNES	20/12/15		Visited 1st & 3rd N.M. field ambulances. Called on D.D.T.S.T. in reference R.R. supply of sergeants. W/d the field ambulance on & arrived at Serge James.	
"	21/12/15		Called at 1st, 2nd & 3rd N.M. field ambulances. Called on A.D.M.S. & arranged to return Sergt James R.R. base; he was however evacuated to same day on account of sickness.	
"	22/12/15		Went to D.ns H.Q. with A.D.M.S. & received instructions to leave by road for HAVRE with all the ambulances on 24th & got bus on 26th. Requested to advise M.T. depot not to send any more stores but to hold on march a parade of workshop when to be called for.	

Army Form C. 2118.

WAR DIARY
or
INTELLIGENCE SUMMARY.
(Erase heading not required.)

Instructions regarding War Diaries and Intelligence Summaries are contained in F. S. Regs., Part II. and the Staff Manual respectively. Title pages will be prepared in manuscript.

Place	Date	Hour	Summary of Events and Information	Remarks and references to Appendices
MINGOVAL	12.3.16		Took Major Freedom to MINGOVAL & secured a farm for the workshop. Bought new R unit in the afternoon. Bought in R Ambulances which had had an accident & which was hanging over the side of a culvert.	
"	13.3.16		Called on 1/3 F.A. at ACQ. Asked Colonel Allen to procure me a fatigue party to clean up my farm which had been left in a disgusting state by the French. Sunbeam Ambulance A9706 broke a cam shaft. This keeps R 4 similar cars in 6 days.	
"	14.3.16		Obtained a fatigue party, Indented wagon & horse from R.E. Mining Co. & cleaned up R yard. 6 Ambulances & 2 Cars all with damaged back axles & 6 of them with broken cam wheels.	
"	15.3.16		Always worse. 10 Cars under repair.	
"	16.3.16		"	
"	17.3.16		A.D.M.S. visited R workshop.	
"	18.3.16		Sent Cars from field ambces at AUBIGNY. Paid 1/1st F.Amb. at ACQ & 1/3rd F.Amb. at ECOIVRES. Called on D.A.D.O.S.	
"	19.3.16		Paid 1/2nd N.M. F.Amb. at VILLIERS CHATEL	
"	20.3.16		Visited & made out the return ambulances have. Plans to get R advance drawing together.	
"	21.3.16		Visited 1/1st & 1/3rd field ambulances.	

WAR DIARY or INTELLIGENCE SUMMARY

Army Form C. 2118.

Place	Date	Hour	Summary of Events and Information	Remarks and references to Appendices
ST VENNANT	10.12.15		Exchanged R 3 ton Halford stores lorry for a Peerless stores lorry in exchange at MERVILLE. Exchanged R Daimler car for a sunken car from R Labou FA.W.U. Also R Lynx at LILLERS. Received advice from DDof S oF 1st Army re 12 Rolhes Ambulance vans R to exchanged for a sunken car from R 19th Div FA + W.U.	
"	11.12.15		Took R remaining Rolhes Ambulances to R Tobacco factory at LOCON + exchanged it for a sunken car from R 19th Div FA+WU. This completed all R exchanges directed to be carried out. In every case R drivers were retained in their respective units. Received a reinforcement of 9 drivers which brought our strength up to establishment.	
"	12.12.15		Inspected horses (donors) of 2nd NM field ambulance + also workshop from him return field dressings etc. Went through stock of materials + ordered any necessary additions.	
"	13.12.15		Went to STEENBECQUE + obtained spun steel. Visited R 3rd NM field ambulance	
"	14.12.15		Went to ISBERGUES + got steel R to be cut for one of R Ford ambulances. Very advisable R mobile field army E R turns taken in obtaining spun steel from R base. Obtained survey form field cashier at MERVILLE + paid R drivers of R 2nd + 3rd NM field ambulances, also workshop men.	
"	15.12.15		Paid drivers of 1st NM F.A. Went with R ADMS R road R railway station at BERGUETTE +	

Army Form C. 2118.

WAR DIARY
or
INTELLIGENCE SUMMARY.
(Erase heading not required.)

Instructions regarding War Diaries and Intelligence Summaries are contained in F. S. Regs., Part II. and the Staff Manual respectively. Title pages will be prepared in manuscript.

Place	Date	Hour	Summary of Events and Information	Remarks and references to Appendices
Sheet 20 16.				
L.12.a.N.W. Sheet 27. 1.140.000	26.7.15	10 A.M.	I arrived at this position at 10.A.M. with the workshops and proceeded to get ready for repairing Gun Tubes &c. Iron Tunis in Bivouac. Weather fine.	
"	27.7.15		Carried out repairs as usual. Weather fine.	
"	28.7.15		" " " " " "	
"	29.7.15		" " " " " The Germans placed 22 shells into the town of POPERINGHE this morning, 11 of which burst.	
"	30.7.15		Removed at 4.12.a N.W. Carrying out necessary repairs	
"	31.7.15		" " " " " " I took a repair lorry up near the dressing station in order to repair an Ambulance as quickly as possible, as they were being used a great deal after late action at HOOGE.	

G.Y. Durward
2/Lt.A.S.C.
O. C. 46th F. A. W. U.

Date................

WAR DIARY or INTELLIGENCE SUMMARY

Army Form C. 2118.

Place	Date	Hour	Summary of Events and Information	Remarks and references to Appendices
ST VENANT	8/12/15		Would be issued through Corps Head Quarters. Tried to find a lathe necessary for workshops with little success. Obtained a forge casting from a foundry at FOUQUEREUIL & made a makeshift of different type which I had had in hand having been unable to obtain a new part in reasonable time from Advance MT Base. Received instructions from DDof S of T 1st Army that the 12 Wolseley Ambulances were to be sent to R Grads New FA 9 WU in exchange for 12 Sunbeam ambulances. That the Daimler Cars now on C/C and C/O Lahore FA 9 WU in exchange for a Sunbeam. That the 2 Triumph Motor Cycles now to be sent to B 38th FA 9 WU in exchange for 2 Douglas ditto. That orders would be issued to this effect through Corps Head Quarters.	
"	9/12/15		New FA 9 WU & arranged for exchange of Ambulances in the following manner. Obtained the Wolseley ambulance from the 3 field Ambulances & took them to MERVILLE where they were handed over to R O C & Grads New FA 9 WU & took over the Sunbeam Ambulances. Only 11 were exchanged as the back axle of one of the Sunbeams was unsafe for a long haul. Later received instructions from DD of S of T 1st Army to exchange the 12th Ambulances for a Sunbeam from the Lahore FA 9 WU. 30 cwt Halford went to BETHUNE & were then & were exchanged for a 30 cwt Daimler from R 20th DSC	

WAR DIARY or INTELLIGENCE SUMMARY

Army Form C. 2118.

Place	Date	Hour	Summary of Events and Information	Remarks and references to Appendices
LA HAIE FARM	15.2.16		Called on Field Cashier, Ordnance & ADMS at PONT REMY. Went to Advanced M.T. Base & obtained a pail for a Ford Ambulance for which I had been waiting for a fortnight.	
"	16.2.16		Ordinary routine. Received instructions from ADMS reconnoitre EPECAMPS & FRANSU for billets for workshops.	
"	17.2.16		Went to EPECAMPS & FRANSU & look for billets for workshop. Found nothing at all suitable at former place but two suitable places at FRANSU. Went to PONT REMY & called on DADMS about missfield ambulance of 1/2nd N.M. Field Ambulance.	
"	18.2.16		Ordinary routine.	
"	19.2.16		Went with Major Dickens of 138th Brigade Staff to BERNAVILLE & there selected a billet for the workshops.	
"	20.2.16		Ordinary routine. Packed up ready for leaving in the morning.	
BERNAVILLE	21.2.16		Moved workshops to a farm at BERNAVILLE & arranged shelters etc. Called on 1/3rd N.M.F.A. at MESNIL.	
"	22.2.16		Went to ABBEVILLE to M.T. School & to buy some chain.	
"	23.2.16		Called on 1/3rd N.M. Field Ambulance at BERNEUIL & on DADMS at RIBEAUCOURT	
"	24.2.16		Called on 1/3rd " " " at MAISON ROLLAND & another section at MESNIL-DOMQUEUR	
"	25.2.16		" " 1/2nd " " " at VACQUERIE. Much snow & ambulances get absolute difficulty.	
"	26.2.16		Drew cash from Field Cashier at BERNAVILLE. Went to N.C. 1/2nd & 1/3rd field ambulances & fuel & drivers, also paid for men of the workshop. Promoted A/L king Sergeant at 1st Drummer Lance Corporal.	

WAR DIARY
or
INTELLIGENCE SUMMARY.
(Erase heading not required.)

Army Form C. 2118.

Place	Date	Hour	Summary of Events and Information	Remarks and references to Appendices
LOCON	1.12.15		Usual routine work, repairs etc.	
"	2.12.15		Completed the repairs to broken down spare lorry & brought it back to depot	
"	3.12.15		Usual routine work, repairs etc	
"	4.12.15		" " " Spare lorry went to MERVILLE for Ordnance & MT Stores on its way back it got stuck in deeply flooded road at PARADIS	
"	5.12.15		Went to see the spare lorry & found that several other lorries were in the same condition also by. Towed it out with R. 1st Aid lorry of a supply column	
"	6.12.15		Usual routine work, repairs etc. About 8 p.m. received a request from DDT/ST, 1st Army for full details of Ambulances, lorries etc. in the unit. Sent this in by road to AIRE the same evening. Later received instructions from R. ADMS & now D.R. Peure at ST. VENNANT	
ST. VENNANT	7.12.15		Went in the morning to see the place allotted which was a corner of a square with no conveniences at all for workshops. Then I found a better vacant place with no conveniences Workshop etc moved over in the afternoon. Secured billets to be seen of for self. Received notification from the DDT/ST, 1st Army that on 3rd Instant Stove lorry was to be sent to 20th ASP in exchange for a 3-Ton Peerless & he got from him at that was 30 cwt Halford was to be sent to 20th DSC in exchange for a 30 cwt Daimler. Also that orders to this effect	

WAR DIARY
or
INTELLIGENCE SUMMARY.

(Erase heading not required.)

Army Form C. 2118.

Place	Date	Hour	Summary of Events and Information	Remarks and references to Appendices
AILLY-LE-HAUT-CLOCHER	8.2.16		Called on 1/1 WM Field Ambulance	
"	9.2.16		Called on Supply Column & arranged for the S. Dwained team cars & took 2 my workshops for all rations & inspection.	
"	10.2.16		Ordinary routine	
"	11.2.16		Received a wire about 8.30 p.m. from A.D.M.S. instructing me to move to workshops the night to LA HAYE Farm near DOMAS which I carried out	
LA HAYE FARM	12.2.16		Called on A.D.M.S. at PONT REMY & found out if I was to stay at LA HAYE Farm. I gathered that I was to stay there & that the move was owing to the village of AILLY being cleared of other troops the 138th Brigade being isolated from a second Receiving Station. Two ambulances a motor car which had been left on the preceding night with ten both cases down were removed to my side. Sixteen cash from Field Cashier at AILLY & paid the men of all 3 Field Ambulances & of the workshop. Called on A.D.M.S. again & explain my arrangement about the motorcycles which he approved of.	
"	13.2.16		Began the system of every ambulance coming to workshops each in a certain day & well fortnight according to 3rd Army Routine order.	
"	14.2.16		Ordinary routine.	

Army Form C. 2118.

WAR DIARY
or
INTELLIGENCE SUMMARY.
(Erase heading not required.)

Instructions regarding War Diaries and Intelligence Summaries are contained in F. S. Regs., Part II. and the Staff Manual respectively. Title pages will be prepared in manuscript.

Place	Date	Hour	Summary of Events and Information	Remarks and references to Appendices
	Sheet No. 12.			
ST. JANS CAPPEL	16/6/15		Remained at ST. JANS CAPPEL Carrying out usual repairs	
"	17/6/15		" " " " " " "	
"	18/6/15		" " " " " " "	
"	19/6/15		" " " " & finished 2nd patent Stretcher Carrier.	
"	20/6/15		" " " " " "	
"	21/6/15		Left this morning on 5 days leave to England.	
"	22/6/15		On leave	
"	23/6/15		On leave	
"	24/6/15		On leave	
"	25/6/15		Returned to ST. JANS CAPPEL from leave.	
ST. JANS CAPPEL	26/6/15		Went in car to look for new situation for Workshops in new area.	
			near POPERINGE.	
"	27/6/15		Rec'd order from A.D.M.S. to move as soon as Waterproof material	
			was obtained for huts for my men.	
"	28/6/15		Remained at ST. JANS CAPPEL carrying out repairs to Ambulances	
			Roads terrible round YPRES & Cars got badly damaged.	

Army Form C. 2118.

WAR DIARY
or
INTELLIGENCE SUMMARY.
(Erase heading not required.)

Instructions regarding War Diaries and Intelligence Summaries are contained in F. S. Regs., Part II. and the Staff Manual respectively. Title pages will be prepared in manuscript.

Place	Date	Hour	Summary of Events and Information	Remarks and references to Appendices
ST. JANS CAPPEL	Sheet No 14.			
	2.7.15		Remained at ST. JANS CAPPEL & carried out necessary repairs	
" "	3.7.15		" " " " " "	
" "	4.7.15		" " " " " "	
" "	5.7.15		" " " " " "	
" "	6.7.15		" " " " " "	
" "	7.7.15		Received orders to proceed to a Farm on Sheet 27. L.23.8.N.E. 1:40,000	
Sheet 27.L.23.8. N.E. 1:40,000			Left ST. JANS CAPPE at 8.30.A.M. Weather fine. Arrived at L.2.3.8.NE at 10.A.M. Put up Bivouacs for the men in a field.	
" "	8.7.15		Started working again today on repairs to the Ambulances.	
" "	9.7.15		Remained carrying out necessary repairs.	
" "	10.7.15		" " " "	
" "	11.7.15		" " " " Major Hutchinson. A.S.C	
" "	12.7.15		Called and made a further inspection of the Workshops.	

WAR DIARY
INTELLIGENCE SUMMARY
(Erase heading not required.)

Army Form C. 2118.

Place	Date	Hour	Summary of Events and Information	Remarks and references to Appendices
ST: VENNANT	8.12.15		Went to Second Army Corps Head Quarters. Tried to find a filter casing spout for workshops with little success. Obtained a bronze casting from a foundry at FOUQUEREUIL & had a new half of differential tube which I had put in hand having been unable to obtain a new part in reasonable time from advance MT base. Received notification from DD of S+T 2nd Army that 2 R 12 Napier Ambulances were to be sent to Corps Siege FA&WU in exchange for 12 Sunbeam ambulances that R Daimler Cars were to be sent to R Lahore FA&WU in exchange for 6 Sunbeam that R 2 Triumph Motor Cycles were to be sent to R 38th FA&WU in exchange for 2 Douglas ditto that orders would be issued to this effect through Corps Head Quarters. Went to R R Grade Siege FA&WU & arranged for exchange of Ambulances on the following morning.	
"	9.12.15		Obtained the Napier ambulances from the 3 field ambulances & took them to MERVILLE where they were handed over to R.O.C. of Grade Siege FA&WU & took over the Sunbeam Ambulances. Only 11 were exchanged as the back axle of one of the Sunbeams was unfit for a stay pad. Later received instructions from DD of S+T 1st Army to exchange the 12 ambulances for a Sunbeam from the Lahore FA&WU. 30 cwt Halford went to BETHUNE square where it was exchanged for a 30 cwt Daimler from the 20th D.S.C.	

Army Form C. 2118.

WAR DIARY
or
INTELLIGENCE SUMMARY.
(Erase heading not required.)

Instructions regarding War Diaries and Intelligence Summaries are contained in F. S. Regs., Part II. and the Staff Manual respectively. Title pages will be prepared in manuscript.

Place	Date	Hour	Summary of Events and Information	Remarks and references to Appendices
LE HAVRE	1.1.16		Received instruction to stand in readiness to embark to-day. Called in ADT at 10.A.M. about 12 mid-day. Embarkation suspended. Sent broken down Sunbeam ambulances nos. 15331 & 15332 & 365 M.T. Co	
"	2.1.16		Ordinary routine	
"	3.1.16		"	
"	4.1.16		"	
"	5.1.16		"	
"	6.1.16		Received instructions at 3 o'clock to entrain at 7.30. Called at AOMG & Base headquarters for further instructions. Called on DADRT. Inspected station & arranged for a crane to be kept in readiness to lift off bodies of ambulances as slung being too high for the gauge. Reached the station. Found 1 at 7.30 & proceeded to load up ambulances etc on trucks. Completed loading at 3 A.M. Train left HAVRE at 3.0 p.m.	
On Rail	7.1.16		Where tea was provided for men. Train crossed 1 Attacks for officer, 28 M., 2 k with orderly station. Reached NANTES 7.59. Picked up 2 DF	
"	8.1.16		On rail. Reached PARAY-LE-MONIAL where tea was provided. 2 men left behind by steward Director at latter place	
MARSEILLES	9.1.16		Arrived at midday. Unloaded 4.30. Got to BORELY PARK 6 o'clock & parked ambulances at back of museum.	

WAR DIARY or INTELLIGENCE SUMMARY

Army Form C. 2118.

Place	Date	Hour	Summary of Events and Information	Remarks and references to Appendices
ST. VENANT	16/12/15		LILLERS in view of the coming interment of those stationed. Went to LILLERS & found out what taken was available for lifting the bodies of Workshop & Store lorries on 2 Railway trucks. Two MT drivers arrived from ROUEN	
"	17.12.15		General routine work	
"	18.12.15		Received information as to men to follow day. Went to THIENNES & inspected the place of permanent arrival for GHQ & also (?) 3rd N.M. field ambulance. Went to THIENNES & placed the workshop in a space made good a site outside this what was not attached to Gen.	
"	19/12/15			
THIENNES	20/12/15		Moved 1st & 3rd N.M. field ambulances. Called on DD.DTS & referred & R ample designs with R field ambulance on & arrival of Segnt forman. Called at 1st, 2nd & 3rd N.M. field ambulances. Called on ADMS & arranged to return staff from R R here; he was however evacuated to same day on account of sickness	
"	21.12.15			
"	22.11.15		Went to DHQ and ADMS & received instructions & leave by road for HAVRE with all the ambulances on 24th & get them to R.E. 26th. Requested to charge MT Depot not to send any more cycles to I.C.R. till so much no trouble of workshop others to called (?)	

Army Form C. 2118.

Army Form C. 2118.

WAR DIARY
or
INTELLIGENCE SUMMARY.
(Erase heading not required.)

Instructions regarding War Diaries and Intelligence Summaries are contained in F. S. Regs., Part II. and the Staff Manual respectively. Title pages will be prepared in manuscript.

Place	Date	Hour	Summary of Events and Information	Remarks and references to Appendices
MARSEILLES	10.1.16		Routine work	
"	11.1.16		Saw numbers of our Base classes of Staff & men	
"	12.1.16		Ordinary routine	
"	13.1.16		" "	
"	14.1.16		Went R for office at Hangar 8 at Docks where HQ moved S wire S	
"	15.1.16		Returns for R hurried missing ships. Ordinary routine	
"	16.1.16		Received some R/R missing mails. The first since leaving HAVRE. Received instructions from Col Allen in R morning that 7 mule ambulances were to embark on R following day with R remains of R 1/2 NM Field Ambulance. Later received further orders R R divis of R 2nd section of ambulances to stand by. Later received instructions that they would not leave for R present a wait further orders.	
"	17.1.16		Ordinary routine	
"	18.1.16		" "	
"	19.1.16		" "	
"	20.1.16		" "	

WAR DIARY
or
INTELLIGENCE SUMMARY.
(Erase heading not required.)

Army Form C. 2118.

Place	Date	Hour	Summary of Events and Information	Remarks and references to Appendices
HINGOVAL	22.3.16		Ordinary routine.	
"	23.3.16		Called in DADT at ST POL re French lumbers Ambulance Convoy which took charge of evacuation etc. I had had made B God an Advance orders & giving methods evacuation made.	
"	24.3.16		Took my learning of ADMS who asked me to arrange for one of B's altered Ford to take him to B's Enterence will B DDMS this afternoon. B Hulwhn went in him.	
"	25.3.16		Went with BDMS & inspected roads for use of Ambulances in case of a heavy attack.	
"	26.3.16		Ordinary routine.	
"	27.3.16		" Supplied Captain ached 10/3/16	
"	28.3.16		" Send R Ambulance 1 man sent on leave PE Stanton	
"	29.3.16		Visited 1/1 MM Field Ambulance	
"	30.3.16		Ordinary routine	
"	31.3.16		"	

D. Young Capt ASC
O C 4/5 DivFAMT

Army Form C. 2118.

WAR DIARY
or
INTELLIGENCE SUMMARY.
(Erase heading not required.)

Instructions regarding War Diaries and Intelligence Summaries are contained in F. S. Regs., Part II. and the Staff Manual respectively. Title pages will be prepared in manuscript.

Place	Date	Hour	Summary of Events and Information	Remarks and references to Appendices
GOSNAY	5.11.15		I left the 15th Divisional Supply Column which was parked at LILLERS & joined my new unit, the 46th Divisional Field Ambulance & Workshop Unit & reported to R ADMS. Col Beevor. The workshops are billeted in the school yard at GOSNAY. Called on Major Turner & inspected the ambulances of the 2nd Field Ambulance at VERQUIN	
"	6.11.15		Went with ADMS to Div HQ at LESTREM. Went on to St OMER & obtained a new radiator for his transhall car	
"	7.11.15		Searched for a suitable billet for the workshops in the new Divisional area. Called at Div HQ & the R ADMS & arranged to defer moving from the present position for the time being	
"	8.11.15		Called upon the ADMS at LESTREM & ascertained the position of the field Ambulance. Drew 6840 francs for pay from the Field Cashier at VAUDRICOURT. Paid the workshop men.	
"	9.11.15		Visited the 1st NM field Ambulance at VIELLE CHAPPELLE, the 2nd do at BUSNES & the 3rd do at ZELOBES. Paid the men at all three places, inspected the ambulances & impressed upon the sergeant the necessity for great cleanliness. Called on R ADMS at LESTREM	
"	10.11.15		Went to England on leave	
"	20.11.15		Returned from leave	

Army Form C. 2118

WAR DIARY
or
INTELLIGENCE SUMMARY.
(Erase heading not required.)

Instructions regarding War Diaries and Intelligence Summaries are contained in F. S. Regs., Part II. and the Staff Manual respectively. Title pages will be prepared in manuscript.

Place	Date	Hour	Summary of Events and Information	Remarks and references to Appendices
Shet. No. 20.				
Shet 27.Farm L. 29. a6.	1.9.15	10.30 A.M.	I arrived at this place and proceeded to arrange my workshops ready for repairs. Also shelters had to be made for the men. Weather was dull and rain at times.	
"	2.9.15		Proceeded to carry out necessary repairs to Ambulances.	
	3.9.15		Usual routine today. Weather very wet.	
	4.9.15		Left for BOULOGNE at 12 noon as I was going on leave	
	5.9.15		On leave of absence.	
	6.9.15		" " " "	
	7.9.15		" " " "	
	8.9.15		" " " "	
	9.9.15		" " " "	
	10.9.15		" " " "	
	11.9.15		" " " Arrived at BOULOGNE 11.30 p.m	
	12.9.15		Returned to my Unit at 1.30 p.m.	
	13.9.15		Usual work on the Ambulances. Weather fine.	" "
	14.9.15		" " " " " "	" "

Army Form C. 2118.

WAR DIARY
or
INTELLIGENCE SUMMARY.
(Erase heading not required.)

Instructions regarding War Diaries and Intelligence Summaries are contained in F.S. Regs., Part II and the Staff Manual respectively. Title pages will be prepared in manuscript.

Sheet No. 8.

Place	Date	Hour	Summary of Events and Information	Remarks and references to Appendices
ST. JANS. CAPELLE	16.4.15		Remained at St. JANS CAPELLE and did necessary repairs.	
"	17.4.15		" " " " " " " "	
"	18.4.15		" " " " " " " "	
"	19.4.15		" " " " " " " "	
"	20.4.15		" " " " " " " "	
"	21.4.15		" " " " " " " "	
"	22.4.15	10.30 p.m.	Received the order to get workshops packed up ready for a sudden move. This order was carried out.	
"	23.4.15		Remained ready to move on receiving the order.	
"	24.4.15		" " " " " "	
"	25.4.15		Started doing repairs again today.	
"	26.4.15		Remained at St. JANS CAPELLE doing necessary repairs	
"	27.4.15		" " " " " "	
"	28.4.15		" " " " " "	
"	29.4.15		" " " " " "	
"	30.4.15		" " " " " "	

J.F. Durward
2/Lieut. A.S.C.
O.C. N.M.F.A. + Unit.

Army Form C. 2118.

WAR DIARY
or
INTELLIGENCE SUMMARY.

(Erase heading not required.)

Instructions regarding War Diaries and Intelligence Summaries are contained in F.S. Regs., Part II. and the Staff Manual respectively. Title pages will be prepared in manuscript.

4th Co. CIV. F.A.W.U.
Date...........
No............

Place	Date	Hour	Summary of Events and Information	Remarks and references to Appendices
Sheet No 17.				
POPERINGHE	1.8.15		Remained here carrying out necessary repairs to Ambulances.	
"	2.8.15		Ditto. Weather fine	
"	3.8.15		Ditto. The town was shelled today, but very little damage done.	
"	4.8.15		Remained doing the usual repairs	
"	5.8.15		" " " "	
"	6.8.15		" " " "	
"	7.8.15		" " " "	
"	8.8.15		" " " "	
"	9.8.15		" " " " Terrific gunfire near YPRES	
"	10.8.15		" " " "	
"	11.8.15		" " " "	
"	12.8.15		" " " "	
"	13.8.15		" " " "	
"	14.8.15		" " " "	
"	15.8.15		" " " "	

Army Form C. 2118.

WAR DIARY
or
INTELLIGENCE SUMMARY.
(Erase heading not required.)

Instructions regarding War Diaries and Intelligence Summaries are contained in F. S. Regs., Part II. and the Staff Manual respectively. Title pages will be prepared in manuscript.

Place	Date	Hour	Summary of Events and Information	Remarks and references to Appendices
	Sheet No. 6.			
CAESTRE	22/3/15		Remained at CAESTRE doing necessary repairs and painting Ambulances Service Colour.	
"	23/3/15		Remained at CAESTRE	
	24/3/15		— ditto —	
	25/3/15		— ditto —	
	26/3/15		— ditto —	
	27/3/15		— ditto —	
	28/3/15		— ditto —	
	29/3/15		— ditto —	
	30/3/15		— ditto —	
	31/3/15		— ditto —	

C.F. Durward 2/Lieut. R.A.M.C.
O.C. North Midland Field
Ambulance (L) Workshop Unit.

WAR DIARY
or
INTELLIGENCE SUMMARY.
(Erase heading not required.)

Army Form C. 2118.

Place	Date	Hour	Summary of Events and Information	Remarks and references to Appendices
AILLY-LE-HAUT-CLOCHER	1.2.16		Inspected the Ambulances of 1/1st N.M. Field Ambulance at PONT REMY & of 1/R 1/1 at "	
"	2.2.16		" 1/3 " " " " "	
"	3.2.16		Received notification of F.G.C.M. to be held next morning. Arranged for witnesses & attend from 1/2nd & 1/3rd N.M. Field Ambulances. Court marital on Lieut. H. Davidson at 10 AM at H.Q. of 138th Inf Bgde. President, Major F.E. Jeffery of 4th Batt. Leicestershire Regt. Members - Capt J.A. BedASE (T.F.) & Lt. H. Hon. R.W. Beckett, Yorkshire Hussars. Concerning officer Bgde General H.S. Campbell, CMG 46th Division. Charges (1) when on active service, drunkenness. (2) When on active service using insubordinate language to his superior officer. Gave evidence. Ordinary routine	
"	4.2.16		" "	
"	5.2.16		Called on acting ADMS at PONT REMY. Received papers with reference to F.G.C.M. on M2 04915-2 Sgy H. Davidson. Finding 'guilty'. To be reduced to 'ranks'. Confirmed by Bgd. General H.S. Campbell & Tuesday day. Promulgated to finding & made necessary entries in conduct sheet & pay book.	
"	6.2.16		With P.S.H. Davidson to ABBEVILLE & sent him to M.E. M.T. Base at ROUEN	
"	7.2.16		Went to the Advance M.T. Base at ABBEVILLE & got huts for which several ambulances were waiting. Called on 3rd N.M. Field Ambulance, inspected the cars & arranged for different work & he need as a rest they had previously been having were knocking much crock up.	

Army Form C. 2118.

WAR DIARY
or
INTELLIGENCE SUMMARY.
(Erase heading not required.)

Instructions regarding War Diaries and Intelligence Summaries are contained in F.S. Regs., Part II. and the Staff Manual respectively. Title pages will be prepared in manuscript.

Place	Date	Hour	Summary of Events and Information	Remarks and references to Appendices
Le HAVRE	1.1.16		Received instructions to stand in readiness to embark 1st day. Called on A.D.T. S.M.A.N. about 12 orderly orderlies and men driver sunbeam ambulances Nos 15331 & 15332 & 386 M.T.C.	
"	2.1.16		Ordinary routine	
"	3.1.16		"	
"	4.1.16		"	
"	5.1.16		"	
"	6.1.16		Received instructions at 3 o'clock to entrain at 7.30. Called on AQMG & Base Headquarters for final instructions. Called on DADRT. Inspected station & arranged for a crane to lift off bodies of workshops & store lorry, being too high for the gauge of return. Pams. & at 7.30 & proceeded & loaded 4 ambulances & on trucks. Reached & station. Pams. & at 3 AM train left HAVRE 7.59. Reached HANTES & 3 J / m Completed loading at 3 AM train left HAVRE 7.59. Reached HANTES & 3 J / m where the men provided for men [illeg] (1 About half an. 2 C.Funds from 28 M. 2 k and orderly serr.	
On Rail	7.1.16		On rail Reached Paray le MONIAL where tea was provided. Rations up.	
"	8.1.16		2 men left behind by & Sherwood Irenhalo. & letter place arrived at midday intimated by 31. GOC & BORELY PARK. 6 o'clock & parked ambulances	
MARSEILLES	9.1.16		I took of horses.	

Army Form C. 2118.

WAR DIARY
or
INTELLIGENCE SUMMARY.
(Erase heading not required.)

Instructions regarding War Diaries and Intelligence Summaries are contained in F.S. Regs., Part II. and the Staff Manual respectively. Title pages will be prepared in manuscript.

Place	Date	Hour	Summary of Events and Information	Remarks and references to Appendices
BERNAVILLE	27.2.16		Called on 1/1st Field Ambulance & told them returning 3 MT drivers to R Base which they were ch. of to having moved the instructions on the subject. Called also on 1/2 & 1/3rd Field Ambulances & finished paying the men at the latter.	
"	28.2.16		Returned all maps to ADMS. Went to DOULLENS. Ordinary Routine	
"	29.2.16		Returned all maps to ADMS. Went to DOULLENS, & which place H.O. had just arrived, & ascertain if there were any movement orders for this unit. Later received orders from ADMS to move to DOULLENS on the following morning & to be clear of BERNAVILLE by 9.30 A.M.	

P.P. String Lieut C.A.S.C.
O.C. 46th Div F.A.W.K.

Army Form C. 2118.

WAR DIARY
or
INTELLIGENCE SUMMARY.
(Erase heading not required.)

Place	Date	Hour	Summary of Events and Information	Remarks and references to Appendices
Sheet N°/3				
ST. JANS CAPPEL.	29/6/15		Remained at ST JANS CAPPEL and carried out necessary repairs.	
"	30/6/15		Major Coulston, Inspector of M.T. came and inspected all the Vehicles of this Unit.	

G. G. Durward
2/Lt. A.S.C. M.T.
O.C. 46th Divnl F.A. Workshop Unit.

1577   Wt. W10791/1773   500,000   1/15   D. D. & L.   A.D.S.S./Forms/C. 2118.

WAR DIARY
or
INTELLIGENCE SUMMARY.

Army Form C. 2118.

(Erase heading not required.)

Place	Date	Hour	Summary of Events and Information	Remarks and references to Appendices
DOULLENS	1.3.16		Left BERNAVILLE at 9 A.M. with lorries & ambulances under orders to rejoin 2nd Army at DOULLENS. Placed workshop in MARCHÉ AU BLÉ	
"	2.3.16		Ordinary routine	
"	3.3.16		"	
"	4.3.16		"	
"	5.3.16		Called on O.C. 42nd Field Ambulance at BEAUVAL. Received orders from A.D.M.S. to move O LE CAUROY on the following day, leaving not later than 1 P.M.	
LE CAUROY	6.3.16		In the morning moved O LE CAUROY & fixed position for the unit with the Camp Commandant. In the afternoon brought unit from DOULLENS O LE CAUROY	
"	7.3.16		Ordinary routine	
"	8.3.16		Went to DOULLENS to see a broken down ambulance. Was forced in the afternoon to obtain a new cylinder head for Sheldon lorry from Supply Column. Sunbeam ambulance AA15187 tested & drawn back	
"	9.3.16		Went to Supply Column SAUBIGNY O find out whether home of lyres which had arrived, were …	
"	10.3.16		Ordinary routine. Received orders to move O CAMBLAIN L'ABBÉ next day aft. 12 Noon. Sunbeam ambulance A17337 fitted to Crossley frame	
CAMBLAIN L'ABBE	11.3.16		Moved O CAMBLAIN L'ABBÉ & fielded lorries & cars in the street. Sunbeam ambulance A17007 fitted to Crossley frame wheel. Sunbeam ambulance 9564 had a hot shaft, damage in back axle from today, the …	

Army Form C. 2118.

WAR DIARY
or
INTELLIGENCE SUMMARY.
(Erase heading not required.)

Instructions regarding War Diaries and Intelligence Summaries are contained in F.S. Regs., Part II. and the Staff Manual respectively. Title pages will be prepared in manuscript.

Place	Date	Hour	Summary of Events and Information	Remarks and references to Appendices
LOCON	27.11.15		Paid drivers of 2nd N.M Field Ambulance & workshop men. Called on DADT 1st army at AIRE with whole returns & enquired whether the motor ambulances detached with the 3 field ambulances should be shown on my returns OR on those of ADMS. Took W.M.M. certificates of GOSNAY.	
"	28.11.15		Called at all 3 field ambulances. The Fodens steam ambulances having in difficulties with frozen hydrogen & very severe weather. Arranged for steam plugs & the steam tubes	
"	29.11.15		Sent spare lorry to HAZEBROUCK to have a wheel retyred. Got a wire in the evening saying the lorry had had a collision. Went & inspected & found the axle of HAZEBROUCK	
"	30.11.15		Sent lorry back & brought back from HAZEBROUCK. ADMS inspected & experimental ambulance lights which I had fitted for him & he instructed me I have the head lamp shades fitted to all the motor ambulances	

P. Strongthur ASC.
OC 46th Div T A & W.U.

AILLY-LE-HAUT-CLOCHER	1.2.16	Inspected Bn ambulances of 1/2nd N.M. Field Ambulance at PONT REMY & of 1/1st
"	2.2.16	" 1/3 "
"		Received notification of FGCM to be held next morning. Arranged for witnesses to attend from 1/2nd & 1/3 NM Field Ambulance
"	3.2.16	Court Martial on Capt H. Sawdon at 10 AM at H.Q. of 138 Inf Bgde. President Major T. Jetley of 4th Batt Lancashire Regt., Members Capt[?] of a Bn A.S.E (T.F.) & 2C.Jc. Hon R.W. Buchell Yorkshire Hussars. Convening officer Bgde. General H.A. Campbell. Capt 4th Seaman. Charges (1) When on active service drunkenness (2) When on active service using imprudent language to his superior officer. Gave evidence. Ordinary routine.
"	4.2.16	
"	5.2.16	Called in acting ADMS at PONT REMY. Received papers not reference to FGCM on Mr 049152 Pay Hr Sawdon. Finding Guilty. To be reduced to be ranks. Confirmed by Bgd General H.A. Campbell & forwarded on. Promulgated to-day. Took necessary action in conduct sheet & pay book & pay book.
"	6.2.16	Took 92. H. Sawdon to ABBEVILLE & sent him off to MT Base at ROUEN
"	7.2.16	Went to the scheme MT Base at ABBEVILLE & got pass for NCOS. several ambulances were ready called on 3rd N.M. Field Ambulance. inspected the cars & arranged for different parts to be used as a load. They had previously been hung up in harbour much cut up.

WAR DIARY
or
INTELLIGENCE SUMMARY.
(Erase heading not required.)

Army Form C. 2118.

Instructions regarding War Diaries and Intelligence Summaries are contained in F.S. Regs., Part II. and the Staff Manual respectively. Title pages will be prepared in manuscript.

Place	Date	Hour	Summary of Events and Information	Remarks and references to Appendices
LA HAIE FARM	15.2.16		Called on Field Cashier. Advance to ADMS at PONT REMY. D of S Advance MT Base at Rouen a Field ambulance for which I had been asked for a fortnight.	
"	16.2.16		Ordinary routine. Received instructions from ADMS of EPECAMPS & FRANSU for billets for workshops.	
"	17.2.8		Went to EPECAMPS & FRANSU & look for billets for workshop. Found nothing at all suitable & furthermore had two suitable places of the latter. Went to PONT REMY & called on ADMS. Also inspected ambulance of 1/2nd WM Field Ambulance.	
"	18.2.16		Ordinary routine.	
"	19.2.16		Went with Major Vickers of 138 Brigade Staff to BERNAVILLE & there selected billet for R workshop.	
"	20.2.16		Ordinary routine. Packed up ready for leaving in R morning.	
BERNAVILLE	21.2.16		Went to workshops to a farm at BERNAVILLE & arranged billets etc. Called on 1/3rd NM FA at MESNIL	
"	22.2.16		Went to ABBEVILLE & MT Sofor – R busy and clean	
"	23.2.16		Called on 1st NM field ambulance at BERNEUIL & on ADMS at RIBEAUCOURT	
"	24.2.16		Called on 1/3rd at MAISON ROLLAND & another section at MESNIL – DOMQUEUR	
"	25.2.16		" " 1/2 " " VACQUERIE trench drain & ambulances gas, also sanitary difficulties	
"	26.2.16		Drew cash from Field Cashier at BERNAVILLE. Went to Mr Hopper 1/1st field ambulances & 1 pack R dinner, also tried R new SR workshop. Purvedier (?) they stripped at the Bernaville Zone exposed	

WAR DIARY or INTELLIGENCE SUMMARY

Army Form C. 2118.

Place	Date	Hour	Summary of Events and Information	Remarks and references to Appendices
AILLY-LE-HAUT-CLOCHER	8.2.16		Called on 1/1 NM Field Ambulance	
"	9.2.16		Called on the supply Column & arranged for the 5 Divisional trans cars to look in on my workshops for all repairs & inspections.	
"			Ordinary routine	
"	10.2.16		" "	
"	11.2.16		Received a wire about 8.30 p.m. from ADMS instructing me to move to workshops HQ my C.R. LA HAYE Farm near DOMAS which I carried out	
LA HAIE FARM	12.2.16		Called on ADMS at PONT REMY & found out I was to stay at LA HAYE Farm. I gathered K.C. I saw & stay there & the R Horse was away & the village of AILLY being cleared of other troops The 138th Brigade being isolated from a receipt of receiving them. Two Ambulances ONE car which had been left on the forecourt high with rear kick axle down were removed to the rear side Draw Cash from Field Cashier at AILLY & found to men of all 3 Field Ambulances a 1 R workshop. Called on ADMS again & explain my arrangements about R motorcycles which he approved of	
"	13.2.16		Began the system of every Ambulance Camp & workshop each as a certain day week in turn of auditing 3rd Army Route order.	
"	14.2.16		Ordinary routine	

WAR DIARY
or
INTELLIGENCE SUMMARY.

Army Form C. 2118.

Place	Date	Hour	Summary of Events and Information	Remarks and references to Appendices
BERNAVILLE	27.2.16		Called on M Field Ambulance & stop them returning 30 T drivers F.A Base which they were abt to S & A.D. having moved R instructions on the subject. Called also on 1/2nd & 1/3rd Field Amb Units & finished paying the men of the Ettn.	
"	28.2.16		Returned all mps of R ADMS Dir of F DOULLENS. Ordinary Routine.	
"	29.2.16		Returned all mps to The ADMS Dir F DOULLENS, R which Place H.Q had just arrived. Excellan. There were any movement orders for these units. Later received orders from ADMS R were to DOULLENS on the following morning as to be clear of BERNAVILLE by 7.30 AM	

P.P. String LinCAsc
O.C. 41 Div F.A.W.K.

Army Form C. 2118.

WAR DIARY
or
INTELLIGENCE SUMMARY.
(Erase heading not required.)

Place	Date	Hour	Summary of Events and Information	Remarks and references to Appendices
Sheet 36 21.				
Sheet 27 40000	15.9.15		Usual routine of repairing Ambulances. Weather fine.	
L 29. a.6.	16.9.15		" " " " dull	
"	17.9.15		" " " " fine	
"	18.9.15		" " " " fine	
"	19.9.15		" " " " fine	
"	20.9.15		" " " " fine	
"	21.9.15		" " " " fine	
"	22.9.15		" " " " dull	
"	23.9.15		" " " " dull	
"	24.9.15		" " " " wet	
"	25.9.15		" " " " dull	
"	26.9.15		" " " " dull	
"	27.9.15		" " " " wet	
"	28.9		" " " " Very wet	
"	29.9		" " " Front Spring Knuckle on my car broke.	
"	30.9		" " " "	

G. C. Durward
2nd Lieut. A.S.C.
O.C. 46th M.A. Workshops Unit

Army Form C. 2118.

WAR DIARY
or
INTELLIGENCE SUMMARY.
(Erase heading not required.)

Instructions regarding War Diaries and Intelligence Summaries are contained in F. S. Regs., Part II. and the Staff Manual respectively. Title pages will be prepared in manuscript.

Place	Date	Hour	Summary of Events and Information	Remarks and references to Appendices
Sheet No 1				
CAESTRE.	1.4.15		Remained at CAESTRE carrying out repairs to Ambulances.	
"	2.4.15		" " " " " " "	
"	3.4.15		" " " " " " "	
"	4.4.15		Packed up Lorries ready to move away from CAESTRE.	
"	5.4.15		Waited for Orders to move.	
"	6.4.15		" " " "	
"	7.4.15		" " " "	
"	8.4.15		" " " "	
"	9.4.15	9.30AM	Left CAESTRE with workshops for St. Jans Capelle.	
St. Jans Capelle		10.30PM	Arrived at ST. JANS CAPELLE and Parked lorries in a brickfield.	
"	10.4.15		Carried out any repairs necessary. Had all lorries thoroughly cleaned.	
"	11.4.15		" " " " " " "	
"	12.4.15		" " " " " " "	
"	13.4.15		" " " " " " "	
"	14.4.15		" " " " " " "	
"	15.4.15		" " " " " " "	

WAR DIARY
or
INTELLIGENCE SUMMARY.
(Erase heading not required.)

Army Form C. 2118.

Place	Date	Hour	Summary of Events and Information	Remarks and references to Appendices
THIENNES	23.12.15		One of the Sunbeam ambulances being stuck up for want of a suitable spare G.R. lorry, a column for which a class R. ST OMER & succeeded in getting one from said place. Received further Sunbeams & Cars others with spares of spring & HAVRE. B.S. of R. ambulances class R. sanitary lorry with R. spare. Left Thiennes for whole journey, 3 days extra return.	
ABBEVILLE	24.12.15		Proceeded to ABBEVILLE with all R. ambulances & lorries of R. unit including R. lorry belonging to R. Sanitary Section. Ford ambulance No 9538 got into a deep ditch on R. way where it was left for R. night. Parked on the road just before getting into R. town	
NEUCHATEL	25.12.15		Drew stores from R.M.T. advance base depot. Left Ford ambulance No.9538 with 317 M.T. Co. Proceeded to NEUCHATEL. Parked m.t. road just before getting into R. town	
Le HAVRE	26.12.15		Proceeded to HAVRE & parked at No 2 rest Camp at SANVIC Routine work.	
"	27.12.15		Routine work	
"	28.12.15		Went to Base M.T. depot at ROUEN & secured main spare parts etc. Received Ford ambulance No 14569 A from GHQ	
"	29.12.15		Being unable to secure no cover sheds for two Sunbeam ambulances with R. p.c. broken, called on A.D.T. & ask if R. ambulances could be replaced	
"	30.12.15		Advised that R. two ambulances were being replaced	
"	31.12.15		Received two Sunbeam ambulances for & from Indian Cavalry Corps.	

H. Strong Lieut A.S.C.
O.C. 4th Div F.A.M.U.

Army Form C. 2118.

WAR DIARY
or
INTELLIGENCE SUMMARY.
(Erase heading not required.)

Instructions regarding War Diaries and Intelligence Summaries are contained in F. S. Regs., Part II. and the Staff Manual respectively. Title pages will be prepared in manuscript.

Place	Date	Hour	Summary of Events and Information	Remarks and references to Appendices
LOCON	1.12.15		Issued routine work, repairs &c.	
"	2.12.15		Emptied the repair & kitchen down stairs lorry & brought it back to R. depot	
"	3.12.15		Issued routine work, repairs &c	
"	4.12.15		Sent tony ward to MERVILLE for exhaust & MT stores	
"	5.12.15		On the way back I got stuck on deeply flooded road at PARADIS. Went & see & show lorry & found hot water ran in the same condition also by Jones. Got out with S. I. and lorry of a supply column	
"	6.12.15		Issued routine work, repairs &c. About 8½ received a report from DDSOT, 1st Army for full details of Ambulances, lorries &c on the road leading to Hay road to AIRE the same evening. Later received instructions from the ADMS to move the Annexe at ST VENNANT	
ST. VENNANT	7.12.15		Went in the morning to see the place allotted which was a corner of the square with no conveniences at all for workshops. Tried to find a better vacant place in the two annexes workshop & moved over in the afternoon. Received letter to the men & for self. Received notification from the DDS+T 1st Army HQ our 3 ton Halford store lorry was to be sent to 20th ASP in exchange for a 3 ton Peerless & to get from him & HQS our 30 cwt Halford Lorry & to send to 20th DSC in exchange for a 30 cwt Daimler. Also the orders to this effect	

WAR DIARY or INTELLIGENCE SUMMARY

Army Form C. 2118.

Place	Date	Hour	Summary of Events and Information	Remarks and references to Appendices
NINGOUAL	12.3.16		Took Major Freedm & MINGOVAL & secured a farm for the workshop. Bought over & went in the afternoon. Bougham & Ambulances which had been in reserve & which was hanging over the rest of sections.	
"	13.3.16		Called on 1/3 F.A. at ACQ. Inspected Colonel Miller & found in a fatigued state & sent up my Van which had been left in a disgusting state by the French Stoneham Ambulance A/708. Broke a Crown wheel. Phosphoney of another case in 8 days.	
"	14.3.16		Obtained a fatigue party. Indent urgently for a front from R.E. having Co. 9 flexened up & got 6 Ambulances & 2 cars all with damaged back axles & 6 of them with broken crown wheels.	
"	15.3.16		Arriving overtime. 10 cars under repair.	
"	16.3.16		" "	
"	17.3.16		" A.D.M.S. visited R. workshop.	
"	18.3.16		New Cook from field Cashier. At AUBIGNY. Paid 1/1st F.Amb. at ACQ. & 1/3rd F.Amb. at ECOIVRES. Called in DADOS.	
"	19.3.16		Paid 1/2nd 149 F.Amb. at VILLERS CHATEL	
"	20.3.16		Visited & rode steed & with Ambulances from Place to 1/3 F.A. advance driving dots.	
"	21.3.16		Visited 4/1st, 4/2nd field ambulances.	

Army Form C. 2118.

WAR DIARY
or
INTELLIGENCE SUMMARY.
(Erase heading not required.)

Place	Date	Hour	Summary of Events and Information	Remarks and references to Appendices
	Sheet 79/0.			
ST. JANS CAPPEL	16/5/15		Remained at ST JANS CAPPEL & carried out necessary repairs	
"	17/5/15		"	
"	18/5/15		"	
"	19/5/15		"	
"	20/5/15		"	
"	21/5/15		"	
"	22/5/15		"	
"	23/5/15		"	
"	24/5/15		"	
"	25/5/15		"	
"	26/5/15		"	
"	27/5/15		"	
"	28/5/15		"	
"	29/5/15		"	
"	30/5/15		"	
"	31/5/15		"	

E.G. Osmond
2/Lt RASC
O/C 46th Divn. F.A.W. Unit

WAR DIARY
or
INTELLIGENCE SUMMARY.

(Erase heading not required.)

Army Form C. 2118.

Place	Date	Hour	Summary of Events and Information	Remarks and references to Appendices
MINGOVAL	22.3.16		Ordinary routine. Called on DADT at ST. POL reference Sunbeam Ambulance Crown wheel	
"	23.3.16		Made drawing of the alteration which I ed had made to Ford Ambulance to give seating accommodation inside.	
"	24.3.16		Took up having to ADMS who asked me to arrange for one of the altered Fords to take him to Conference with DDMS that afternoon.	
"	25.3.16		Deal with ADMS & inspect routes for use of Ambulances in case of a heavy attack	
"	26.3.16		Ordinary routine	
"	27.3.16		" " Inspection Return dated 10/3/16	
"	28.3.16		" " Send R Ambulance. 1 man sent on leave Pte Stanton	
"	29.3.16		Visited 1/1 MM. Field Ambulance.	
"	30.3.16		Ordinary routine	
"	31.3.16		"	

D. H. Young Capt A.S.C.

O.C. 46 Div F.A.W.W.

WAR DIARY or INTELLIGENCE SUMMARY

Army Form C. 2118.

Place	Date	Hour	Summary of Events and Information	Remarks and references to Appendices
MARSEILLES	21.1.16		Sent 7 ambulances & bike sitting cases & the clerks for instruction	
"	22.1.16		Sent 5 ambulances & bring the sitting cases back again	
"	23.1.16		Two men from Base Croker & Tait fell sick.	
"	24.1.16		Ordinary routine. P.C. Sergt. H. Bardoni under arrest for drunkenness - insolent	
"	25.1.16		" Took 7 ambulances to station in evening & entrain with 1st N.M. Field Ambulance	
"	26.1.16		Received orders during the afternoon to entrain on train leaving at 3.12 next morning. Arranged with D.A.D.R.T. & have trucks in readiness under electric cranes for loading the lorries — the ambulances of 3rd N.M. Field Ambulance going by same train. Left for ARENC station at 10.15	
On Rail	27.1.16		Informed that Crane was out of order. Three of the lorries having to be loaded with their bodies in & sprags truck on account of two quick heys, the lorries had to be left behind, & being arranged that they were to come on next morning. Train loaded & ambulances. Train left 5.30 AM	
"	28.1.16		Journey continued	
PONT REMY	29.1.16		Arrived at PONT REMY at 5.30 AM. Unloaded Ambulances. Billeted the men. Handed over to Sergeant under orders of 6 A.P.M. D and Lieut. Col. Walsh E.F. 3rd & 1st N.M. Field Ambulance	
"	30.1.16		Lorries arrived about 5 P.M. had the heavy resp. tackle for unloading them. The trucks were sent on to ABBEVILLE with a fatigue party of 1 hr. Went to AILLY LE HAUT CLOCHER & secured a place for PSO	

Army Form C. 2118.

WAR DIARY
or
INTELLIGENCE SUMMARY.
(Erase heading not required.)

Instructions regarding War Diaries and Intelligence Summaries are contained in F. S. Regs., Part II. and the Staff Manual respectively. Title pages will be prepared in manuscript.

Place	Date	Hour	Summary of Events and Information	Remarks and references to Appendices
Sheet 27 N°15.				
Sheet 27 L.23.b.NE. 1:40.000	13.7.15		Remained at this Farm Carrying out necessary repairs.	
" "	14.7.15		" "	
" "	15.7.15		" "	
" "	16.7.15		" "	
" "	17.7.15		" "	
" "	18.7.15		" "	
" "	19.7.15		" "	
" "	20.7.15		" "	
" "	21.7.15		" "	
" "	22.7.15		" "	
" "	23.7.15		" "	
" "	24.7.15		" "	
" "	25.7.15		Rec'd orders to move to the new area as soon as possible. So proceeded to find a suitable place. Found one near POPERINGHE.	
" "	26.7.15		Left the Farm L.23.b.N.E. Sheet 27. 1:40.000, at 9.30 A.M.	

Army Form C. 2118.

WAR DIARY
or
INTELLIGENCE SUMMARY.
(Erase heading not required.)

Instructions regarding War Diaries and Intelligence Summaries are contained in F. S. Regs., Part II. and the Staff Manual respectively. Title pages will be prepared in manuscript.

Place	Date	Hour	Summary of Events and Information	Remarks and references to Appendices
MARSEILLES	10.1.16		Routine work	
"	11.1.16		Also survey for Base Chevier a fact the men	
"	12.1.16		Ordinary routine	
"	13.1.16		" "	
"	14.1.16		Went to office of Movements at Docks where they promised to use C	
"	15.1.16		Bellagio for the hands moving thence	
"			Ordinary routine	
"	16.1.16		Received some of the missing hands. First snow leaving HARFIT. Received instructions from Col. Allen in the morning that 7 with Ambulances were to embark on the following day with 8 horses of the 1/2 NM Field Ambulance to proceed from there to the service of the 2nd section of Ambulances & stand by. Later received instructions that they would not leave for the present & would further orders.	
"	17.1.16		Ordinary routine	
"	18.1.16		" "	
"	19.1.16		" "	
"	20.1.16		" "	

1577 Wt.W10791/1773 500,000 1/15 D.D.&L. A.D.S.S./Forms/C. 2118.

Army Form C. 2118.

WAR DIARY
or
INTELLIGENCE SUMMARY.
(Erase heading not required.)

Instructions regarding War Diaries and Intelligence Summaries are contained in F.S. Regs., Part II. and the Staff Manual respectively. Title pages will be prepared in manuscript.

Place	Date	Hour	Summary of Events and Information	Remarks and references to Appendices
GOSNAY	21.11.15		Routine work. Saunders car which was overhauled whilst I was on leave was found to have broken differential casing. Car consequently out of action ready for new part.	
"	22.11.15		Visited Nos. 1 & 3rd Field Ambulances & instructed the sergeants as to making returns of the change of Ambulances. Went to see the ADMS at LESTREM but he was out. Went to ISEBERG & obtained a piece of steel to make a back axle shoe of one of the Sunbeam Ambulances, the car having been out of action for very many weeks whilst for a new part from the Base MT depot. Instructed the sergeant to have lighted lamps placed under the bonnet of the Ambulance to guard against frost. Routine work.	
"	23.11.15		Routine work.	
"	24.11.15		Routine work. Paid for Sunbeam Ambulance completed.	
"	25.11.15		Received instructions at 10 o'clock to move the unit to MERVILLE. Called on Major Fairweather at LESTREM who suggested my calling on Major Potter of the Supply Column with regard to finding a suitable situation. Called on Major Potter & scouted all round MERVILLE and could find no suitable moveable place. Later the ADMS suggested a farm at LOCON which I found quite suitable. BETHUNE continued sheet X 7.d.7.7. Sunbeam Ambulance completed as a road ambulance.	
LOCON	26.11.15		Drew money for Field Cashier at MERVILLE. Paid 1 & 3rd Field Ambulances. Fitted up the workshops during first day in the new place.	

Army Form C. 2118.

WAR DIARY
or
INTELLIGENCE SUMMARY.
(Erase heading not required.)

Instructions regarding War Diaries and Intelligence Summaries are contained in F. S. Regs., Part II. and the Staff Manual respectively. Title pages will be prepared in manuscript.

Sheet No. 1.

Place	Date	Hour	Summary of Events and Information	Remarks and references to Appendices
ST. JANS CAPPEL	1/6/15		Stationed at ST. JANS CAPPEL carrying out necessary repairs to Ambulances	
"	2/6/15		" " " " " " " " " " " "	
"	3/6/15		" " " " " " " " " " " "	
"	4/6/15		" " " " " " " " " " " "	
"	5/6/15		" " " " " " " " " " " "	
"	6/6/15		" " " " " " " " " " " "	
"	7/6/15		" " " " " " " " " " " "	
"	8/6/15		" " " " " " " " " " " "	
"	9/6/15		" " " " " " " " " " " "	
"	10/6/15		" " " " " " " " " " " "	
"	11/6/15		" " " " " " " " " " " "	
"	12/6/15		" " " " " " " " " " " "	
"	13/6/15		" " " " " " " " " " " "	
"	14/6/15		" " " " " " " " " " " "	
"	15/6/15		" " " " " " " " " " " "	

WAR DIARY
or
INTELLIGENCE SUMMARY.
(Erase heading not required.)

Army Form C. 21[??]

Instructions regarding War Diaries and Intelligence Summaries are contained in F. S. Regs., Part II. and the Staff Manual respectively. Title pages will be prepared in manuscript.

Place	Date	Hour	Summary of Events and Information	Remarks and references to Appendices
LOCON	27.11.15		Paid drivers of 2nd NM Field Ambulance & Workshop men. Called on DADT & Army at AIRE with whole returns & enquired whether the motor ambulances detached with the 3 field ambulances should be shown on my returns or on those of ADMS. Lough Whitley certificate S. GOSNAY.	
"	28.11.15		Called at all 3 field ambulances. The Ford steam ambulances having no difficulties with frozen [water] own as severe weather. Arranged for them King & the steam [?]pe	
"	29.11.15		Lent spare lorry to HAZEBROUCK to have a wheel retyred. Got a wire in the evening saying the lorry had lost a column. Sent a inspector to find the side of HAZEBROUCK	
"	30.11.15		Bent lorry axle etc. brought back from HAZEBROUCK. ADMS inspected the experimental ambulance lights which I had prepared for him & he instructed me to have the head lamp shades fitted to all the motor ambulances	

P. R. Thorogood A.S.C.
O.C. 46th Div. F.A. Wksp.

Army Form C. 2118.

WAR DIARY
or
INTELLIGENCE SUMMARY.
(Erase heading not required.)

Instructions regarding War Diaries and Intelligence Summaries are contained in F.S. Regs., Part II. and the Staff Manual respectively. Title pages will be prepared in manuscript.

Place	Date	Hour	Summary of Events and Information	Remarks and references to Appendices
AILLY-LE-HAUT-CLOCHER	31.1.16		workshops at a button factory. Moved to AILLY-LE-HAUT-CLOCHER. The lorries were unloaded from trucks at ABBEVILLE station & brought on to former place. This place is centrally placed between 5 their field ambulances	

P H Strong Lt Col
O C 46th Div F A WL

46th Div. F.A.W.U.
R/333

Army Form C. 2118.

WAR DIARY
or
INTELLIGENCE SUMMARY.

(Erase heading not required)

46 FAWU

Place	Date	Hour	Summary of Events and Information	Remarks and references to Appendices
MINADVAL	1.4.11		Field Ambulance Workshop under instructions called on ADMS & on Supply Column railway siding	
	2.4.11		"	
	3.4.11			
	4.4.11			
	5.4.11		Car to spare having been with 3 drivers say 7 carrys Proceeded & whilst formally handed over to 46 Divisional Supply Column	

R. Strong Capt RASC

WAR DIARY
or
INTELLIGENCE SUMMARY.
(Erase heading not required.)

Army Form C. 2118.

Place	Date	Hour	Summary of Events and Information	Remarks and references to Appendices
THIENNES	23.12.15		One of the sunken ambulances being glad up to mend. A full new Ford GS Supply column to rail & also R. ST OMER & succeeded in getting one from each place. Received from R. Snoward & Co, others with spheres of money & with letters for whole group. 3 days extra rations.	
ABBEVILLE	24.12.15		Proceeded to ABBEVILLE with all R. ambulances in convoy of two vans of the unit including the lorry belonging to R. Sanitary section. Ford Ambulance No 9358 got into a deep ditch on the way where it was left for the night. Parked on the road just before getting into town. Drew stores from R. MT advance base depôt. Left Ford Ambulance No 9358 with 317 MT Co.	
NEUCHATEL	25.12.15		Proceeded to NEUCHATEL. Parked on road just before getting into town.	
LE HAVRE	26.12.15		Proceeded to HAVRE & parked at No 2 Rest Camp at SANVIC. Raining with...	
"	27.12.15			
"	28.12.15		Went to Base MT Depot at ROUEN & drew new spare wheels. Received Ford ambulance No 14589 for GHQ	
"	29.12.15		Being unable to secure new cross shafts for two sunken ambulances with the Ford column called on ADT & col of SA ambulance could be effected.	
"	30.12.15 31.12.15		Received... two ambulances... from Indian Cavalry Corps	

H. Strong Lt.?C
OC 46 StAAMTC

Army Form C. 2118.

WAR DIARY
or
INTELLIGENCE SUMMARY.
(Erase heading not required.)

Instructions regarding War Diaries and Intelligence Summaries are contained in F. S. Regs., Part II. and the Staff Manual respectively. Title pages will be prepared in manuscript.

Place	Date	Hour	Summary of Events and Information	Remarks and references to Appendices
Sheet 99 a.				
St. Jans Cappel	1/5/15.		Remained at ST. JANS CAPPEL & carried out necessary repairs to Ambulances.	
"	2/5/15		"	
"	3/5/15		"	
"	4/5/15		"	
"	5/5/15		"	
"	6/5/15		"	
"	7/5/15		"	
"	8/5/15		"	
"	9/5/15		"	
"	10/5/15		"	
"	11/5/15		"	
"	12/5/15		"	
"	13/5/15		"	
"	14/5/15		"	
"	15/5/15		"	

Army Form C. 2118.

WAR DIARY
or
INTELLIGENCE SUMMARY.
(Erase heading not required.)

Instructions regarding War Diaries and Intelligence Summaries are contained in F. S. Regs., Part II. and the Staff Manual respectively. Title pages will be prepared in manuscript.

Place	Date	Hour	Summary of Events and Information	Remarks and references to Appendices
MILLENCOURT	1.4.16		Field Ambulance - Workshop units abolished. Called on ADMS + on Supply Column	
"	2.4.16		Ordinary routine	
"	3.4.16		" "	
"	4.4.16		" "	
"	5.4.16		Car a spare lorry together with 3 drivers sent away	
"	6.4.16		Personnel & vehicles formally handed over to 46th Divisional Supply Column	

P.T. King Capt ASC

1577 Wt.W10791/1773 500,000 1/15 D.D.&L. A.D.S.S./Forms/C.2118.

WAR DIARY
or
INTELLIGENCE SUMMARY.
(Erase heading not required.)

Army Form C. 2118.

Place	Date	Hour	Summary of Events and Information	Remarks and references to Appendices
AILLY-LE-HAUT-CLOCHER	31.1.16		workshops & a butter factory. Moved to AILLY-LE-HAUT-CLOCHER. The lorries were unloaded from trucks at ABBEVILLE station & brought on farther place. This place is centrally placed between 3 other field ambulances.	

P.P. Strong Lt C.
O.C. 46th Div F.A. M.U.

46

46 Div. School Workshops

Jan
Vol XI.

F

Jan 1916

46 Aars.
vol: IX

121/7294

46/H Kristian

Nov. 15.

Nov 1915

Dec/Vol. XI

121/7929

N.M. Field Ambulance Workshop hunt

Vol I

121/6754

46th Division

46th Div: F.A. Workshops Unit

Vol XIII

August 15

WAR DIARY

of

46th Dvisional Field Ambulance Workshop Unit. A.S.C.

March & For April 1916

WO 268 12

181/6250

46th Division

46th Field Amb: Notts&Derby mount

Part VI   1 – 31.7.15

July 1915

46th [Division]

1999/121

46th M. Amb. Workshop Unit

Vol VIII

Sep. 15

Feb 1916

46th (M.U.) yaw.

12/5/95
April 1915

121/5195

121/5195

North Midland. Tel: Amet. No Reply

Vol III

121/5481

46th Divl. Field Ambulance War Diary & war

Vol IV

May 1915.

131/4555

N.M. Division

46th Scottish Lowland F.A: Ambulance Workshop.

Vol III. 1 — 31. 3. 15.

151/5595

46th Division

46. Div: F.A. Workshop
Vol V

June 1915.

46

3d Amb Work Unit
Vol XIV

46th
A. F. a. Amb. Work Unit
Vol I

www.ingramcontent.com/pod-product-compliance
Lightning Source LLC
Chambersburg PA
CBHW081237170426
43191CB00034B/1963